General Instructions

1 Read materials list and instructions for individual tissue cover before beginning.

2 Cut plastic canvas as instructed.

3 Stitch all pieces following individual instructions and graphs. Use #16 tapestry needle when stitching with worsted weight yarn. Use #18 tapestry needle when stitching with metallic needlepoint yarn or 6-strand embroidery floss. When stitching with metallic needlepoint yarn, keep it smooth and flat as you stitch. When stitching with 6-strand embroidery floss, first separate the correct number of strands from a length of floss, then recombine them without twisting.

4 Unless instructed otherwise, add embroidery stitches—Backstitch, Straight Stitch, French Knots, Lazy Daisy Stitch—after background stitching is complete.

5 Whipstitch sides to tops. Whipstitch sides to each other along corners. Overcast unfinished edges as instructed.

6 Add embellishments or stitched panels as instructed.

Cherish

Size: 5 inches W x 5⅝ inches H x 5 inches deep
(12.7cm x 14.3cm x 12.7cm)
Skill Level: Intermediate

Materials

❑ 1½ sheets stiff 7-count plastic canvas
❑ Coats & Clark Red Heart Classic worsted weight yarn Art. E267 as listed in color key
❑ Coats & Clark Red Heart Super Saver worsted weight yarn Art. E300 as listed in color key
❑ DMC 6-strand embroidery floss as listed in color key
❑ Tapestry needles: #16 and #18
❑ Hot-glue gun and glue sticks
❑ 4 (2 x 3-inch) photos

Stitching Step By Step

1 Cut plastic canvas according to graphs. Cut out openings in top and sides.

2 Stitch sides, top and signs according to graphs. Overcast openings in top and sides and edges of signs.

3 When background stitching is complete, Backstitch and Straight Stitch lettering on signs using 6 strands black embroidery floss; Backstitch borders and stripes, taking each stitch over two bars.

4 Whipstitch sides to top and to each other along corners according to graphs. Overcast bottom edge. Using 6 strands black embroidery floss, add black stitches over edges to continue lines.

5 Trim photos to desired size; glue to inside of tissue box cover behind openings.

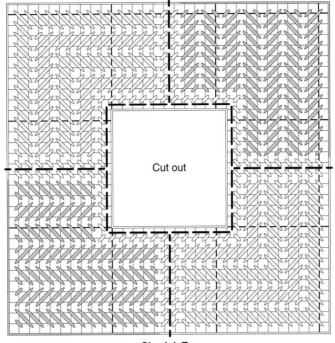

Cherish Top
31 holes x 31 holes
Cut 1

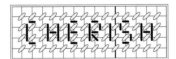

Cherish Sign
15 holes x 5 holes
Cut 4

COLOR KEY	
Yards	**Worsted Weight Yarn**
8 (7.3m)	☐ White #1
15 (13.7m)	☐ Eggnog #329
19 (17.4m)	▨ Pale plum #579
6 (5.5m)	☐ Pale sage #622
	6-Strand Embroidery Floss
7 (6.4m)	✐ Black #310 (6-strand) Backstitch and Straight Stitch

Color numbers given are for Coats & Clark Red Heart Classic worsted weight yarn Art. E267 and Super Saver worsted weight yarn Art. E300 and DMC 6-strand embroidery floss.

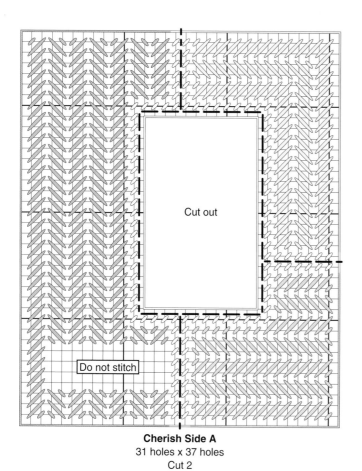

Cherish Side A
31 holes x 37 holes
Cut 2

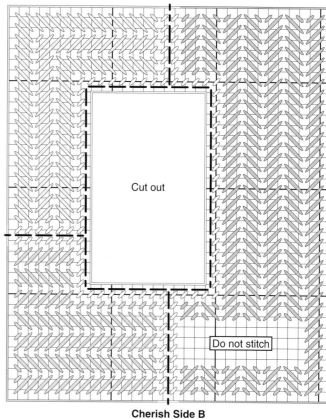

Cherish Side B
31 holes x 37 holes
Cut 2

COLOR KEY	
Yards	**Worsted Weight Yarn**
8 (7.3m)	☐ White #1
15 (13.7m)	☐ Eggnog #329
19 (17.4m)	▨ Pale plum #579
6 (5.5m)	☐ Pale sage #622
	6-Strand Embroidery Floss
7 (6.4m)	✏ Black #310 (6-strand) Backstitch and Straight Stitch

Color numbers given are for Coats & Clark Red Heart Classic worsted weight yarn Art. E267 and Super Saver worsted weight yarn Art. E300 and DMC 6-strand embroidery floss.

Grow

Size: 9⅞ inches W x 3¾ inches H x 5 inches deep
(25.1cm x 9.5cm x 12.7cm)
Skill Level: Intermediate

Materials

- ❏ 1½ sheets stiff 7-count plastic canvas
- ❏ Coats & Clark Red Heart Classic worsted weight yarn Art. E267 as listed in color key
- ❏ Coats & Clark Red Heart Super Saver worsted weight yarn Art. E300 as listed in color key
- ❏ ⅛-inch (4mm) Plastic Canvas 7 Metallic Needlepoint Yarn from Rainbow Gallery as listed in color key
- ❏ DMC 6-strand embroidery floss as listed in color key
- ❏ Tapestry needles: #16 and #18

Stitching Step By Step

1 Cut plastic canvas according to graphs. Cut out opening in top.

2 Stitch sides and top according to graphs, working uncoded areas with soft white Continental Stitches. Overcast opening in top.

3 When background stitching is complete, Backstitch and Straight Stitch lettering and Straight Stitch stems of leaves using 6 strands black embroidery floss. Backstitch stripes on top, sides and ends using 3 strands medium copper embroidery floss, and taking each stitch over two bars.

4 Whipstitch sides and ends to top and to each other along corners according to graphs; Overcast bottom edge.

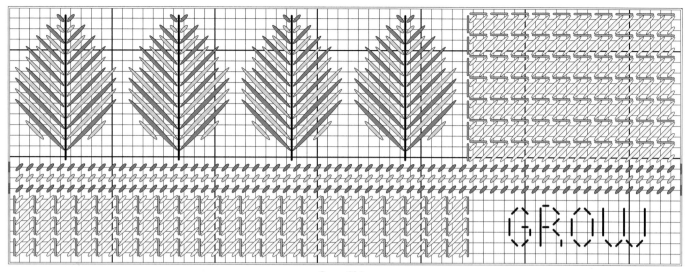

Grow Side
65 holes x 24 holes
Cut 2

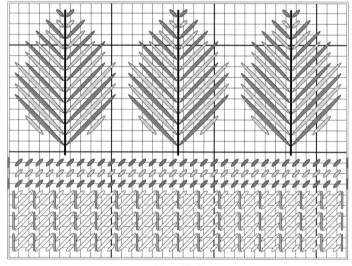

Grow End
33 holes x 24 holes
Cut 2

COLOR KEY	
Yards	**Worsted Weight Yarn**
13 (11.9m)	■ Bronze #286
37 (33.8m)	☐ Eggnog #329
10 (9.1m)	☐ Light thyme #342
10 (9.1m)	■ Medium thyme #406
27 (24.7m)	Uncoded areas are soft white #316 Continental Stitches
	⁄ Soft white #316 Overcasting and Whipstitching
	⅛-Inch (4mm) Metallic Needlepoint Yarn
7 (6.4m)	☐ Gold #PC1
	6-Strand Embroidery Floss
4 (3.6m)	⁄ Black #310 (6-strand) Backstitch and Straight Stitch
7 (6.4m)	⁄ Medium copper #920 (3-strand) Backstitch

Color numbers given are for Coats & Clark Red Heart Classic worsted weight yarn Art. E267 and Super Saver worsted weight yarn Art. E300, Rainbow Gallery Plastic Canvas 7 Metallic Needlepoint Yarn and DMC 6-strand embroidery floss.

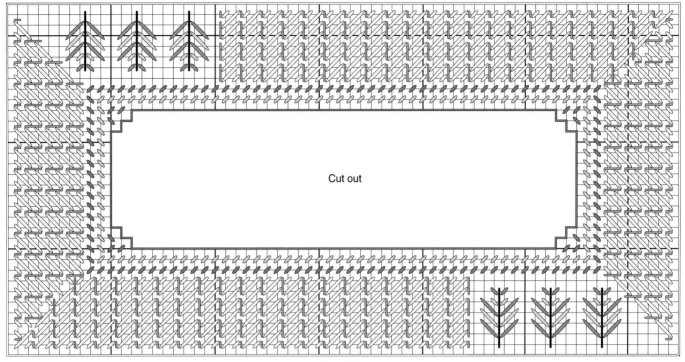

Grow Top
65 holes x 33 holes
Cut 1

COLOR KEY	
Yards	**Worsted Weight Yarn**
13 (11.9m)	■ Bronze #286
37 (33.8m)	☐ Eggnog #329
10 (9.1m)	☐ Light thyme #342
10 (9.1m)	▦ Medium thyme #406
27 (24.7m)	Uncoded areas are soft white #316 Continental Stitches
	⁄ Soft white #316 Overcasting and Whipstitching
	⅛-Inch (4mm) Metallic Needlepoint Yarn
7 (6.4m)	☐ Gold #PC1
	6-Strand Embroidery Floss
4 (3.6m)	✦ Black #310 (6-strand) Backstitch and Straight Stitch
7 (6.4m)	⁄ Medium copper #920 (3-strand) Backstitch

Color numbers given are for Coats & Clark Red Heart Classic worsted weight yarn Art. E267 and Super Saver worsted weight yarn Art. E300, Rainbow Gallery Plastic Canvas 7 Metallic Needlepoint Yarn and DMC 6-strand embroidery floss.

Dream

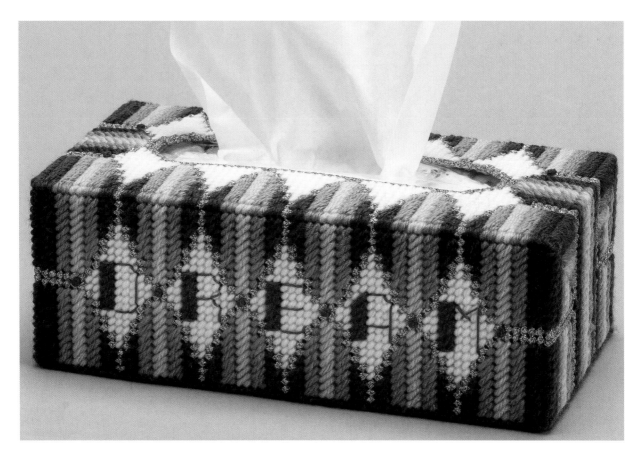

Size: 10 inches W x 3½ inches H x 5⅛ inches deep
(25.4cm x 8.9cm x 13cm)

Skill Level: Intermediate

Materials

- ❏ 1½ sheets stiff 7-count plastic canvas
- ❏ Coats & Clark Red Heart Super Saver worsted weight yarn Art. E300 as listed in color key
- ❏ ⅛-inch (4mm) Plastic Canvas 7 Metallic Needlepoint Yarn from Rainbow Gallery as listed in color key
- ❏ DMC 6-strand embroidery floss as listed in color key
- ❏ Tapestry needles: #16 and #18

Stitching Step By Step

1 Cut plastic canvas according to graphs. Cut out opening in top.

2 Stitch sides, ends and top according to graphs, working uncoded areas with soft white Continental Stitches. Overcast opening in top.

3 When background stitching is complete, add dark plum French Knots to sides, ends and top. Backstitch and Straight Stitch lettering on sides using 6 strands dark violet embroidery floss.

4 Whipstitch sides and ends to top and to each other along corners according to graphs; Overcast bottom edge.

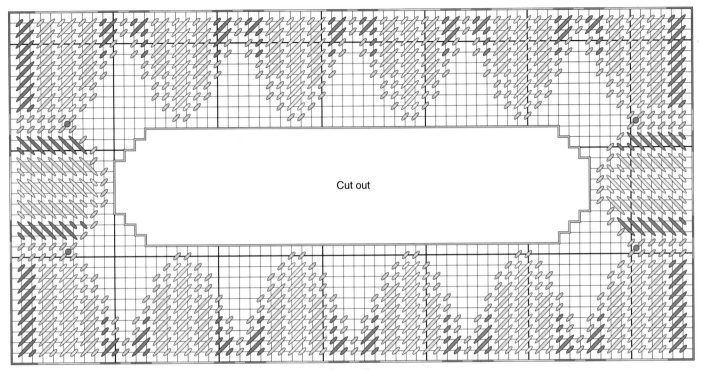

Dream Top
66 holes x 33 holes
Cut 1

COLOR KEY		
Yards		**Worsted Weight Yarn**
28 (25.6m)	☐	Light plum #531
28 (25.6m)	◼	Dark plum #533
19 (17.4m)	☐	Pale plum #579
25 (22.9m)		Uncoded areas are soft white #316 Continental Stitches
	●	Dark plum #533 French Knot
		¹/₈-Inch (4mm) Metallic Needlepoint Yarn
26 (23.8m)	☐	Gold #PC1
		6-Strand Embroidery Floss
4 (3.6m)	╱	Dark violet #327 (6-strand) Backstitch and Straight Stitch

Color numbers given are for Coats & Clark Red Heart Super Saver worsted weight yarn Art. E300, Rainbow Gallery Plastic Canvas 7 Metallic Needlepoint Yarn and DMC 6-strand embroidery floss.

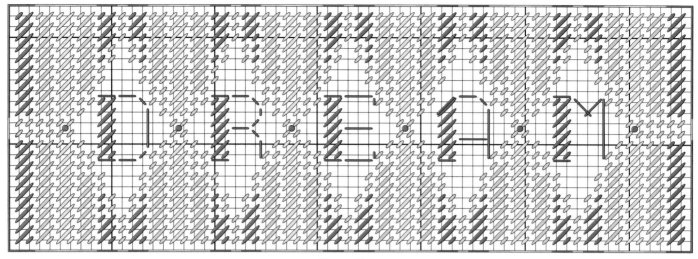

Dream Side
66 holes x 23 holes
Cut 2

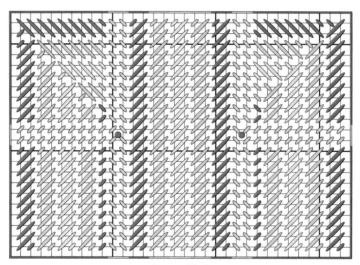

Dream End
33 holes x 23 holes
Cut 2

COLOR KEY		
Yards	**Worsted Weight Yarn**	
28 (25.6m)	☐ Light plum #531	
28 (25.6m)	■ Dark plum #533	
19 (17.4m)	☐ Pale plum #579	
25 (22.9m)	Uncoded areas are soft white #316 Continental Stitches	
	● Dark plum #533 French Knot	
	⅛-Inch (4mm) Metallic Needlepoint Yarn	
26 (23.8m)	☐ Gold #PC1	
	6-Strand Embroidery Floss	
4 (3.6m)	⁄ Dark violet #327 (6-strand) Backstitch and Straight Stitch	

Color numbers given are for Coats & Clark Red Heart Super Saver worsted weight yarn Art. E300, Rainbow Gallery Plastic Canvas 7 Metallic Needlepoint Yarn and DMC 6-strand embroidery floss.

Smile

Size: 5¾ inches W x 6½ inches H x 5¾ inches deep
  (14.6cm x 16.5cm x 14.6cm)

Skill Level: Intermediate

Materials

- ❏ 1½ sheets clear 7-count plastic canvas
- ❏ Coats & Clark Red Heart Classic worsted weight yarn Art. E267 as listed in color key
- ❏ Coats & Clark Red Heart Super Saver worsted weight yarn Art. E300 as listed in color key
- ❏ Coats & Clark Red Heart Kids worsted weight yarn Art. E711 as listed in color key
- ❏ DMC 6-strand embroidery floss as listed in color key
- ❏ Tapestry needles: #16 and #18
- ❏ Hot-glue gun and glue sticks

Stitching Step By Step

1 Cut plastic canvas according to graphs.

2 Stitch sides, signs and corner strips. Overcast signs.

3 When background stitching is complete, add orange French Knots to flower centers. Backstitch and Straight Stitch lettering on signs and add French Knot dots to i's using 6 strands black embroidery floss.

4 Whipstitch corner strips to sides, beginning at bottom and bending pieces as needed to form curves at top. Overcast center opening and bottom edges according to graphs.

5 Hot-glue signs over unstitched areas on sides.

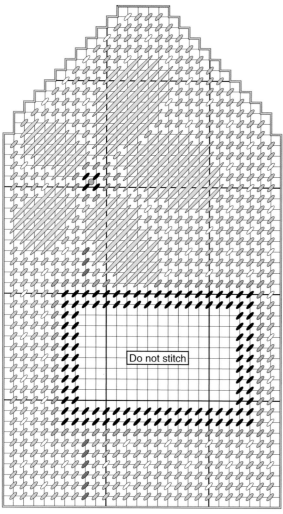

Smile Side
27 holes x 47 holes
Cut 4

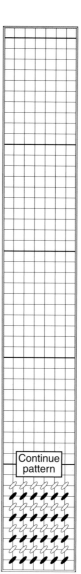

Smile Corner Strip
7 holes x 51 holes
Cut 4

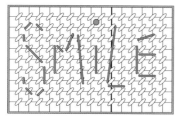

Smile Sign
16 holes x 10 holes
Cut 4

COLOR KEY

Yards	Worsted Weight Yarn
27 (24.7m)	☐ White #1
18 (16.4m)	■ Black #12
13 (11.9m)	☐ Bright yellow #324
2 (1.8m)	☐ Paddy green #686
7 (6.4m)	☐ Orange #2252
38 (34.7m)	☐ Lime #2652
6 (5.5m)	☐ Pink #2734
	● Orange #2252 French Knot

6-Strand Embroidery Floss

4 (3.6m)	╱ Black #310 (6-strand) Backstitch and Straight Stitch
	● Black #310 (6-strand) French Knot

Color numbers given are for Coats & Clark Red Heart Classic worsted weight yarn Art. E267, Super Saver worsted weight yarn Art. E300 and Kids worsted weight yarn Art. E711, and DMC 6-strand embroidery floss.

Live, Laugh, Love

Size: 4⅞ inches W x 5¾ inches H x 4⅞ inches deep
(12.4cm x 14.6cm x 12.4cm)
Skill Level: Intermediate

Materials

- ❏ 1½ sheets stiff 7-count plastic canvas
- ❏ ½ sheet ivory 7-count plastic canvas
- ❏ Coats & Clark Red Heart Classic worsted weight yarn Art. E267 as listed in color key
- ❏ ⅛-inch (4mm) Plastic Canvas 7 Metallic Needlepoint Yarn from Rainbow Gallery as listed in color key
- ❏ DMC 6-strand embroidery floss as listed in color key
- ❏ Tapestry needles: #16 and #18
- ❏ 16 (⅝-inch/1.6cm) Tulip See-Thru Stones
- ❏ Hot-glue gun and clear-drying glue sticks

Stitching Step By Step

1 Cut plastic canvas according to graphs, cutting sides and top from clear plastic canvas and signs from ivory plastic canvas. Cut out opening in top.

2 Stitch sides, top and signs. Overcast opening in top; signs are not Overcast.

3 When background stitching is complete, Backstitch and Straight Stitch lettering on signs and add French Knot dots to i's using 6 strands black embroidery floss.

4 Whipstitch sides to top and to each other along corners according to graphs; Overcast bottom edge.

5 Hot-glue signs over unstitched areas on sides. Hot-glue see-through stones over metallic gold Slanted Gobelin stitches on sides and top.

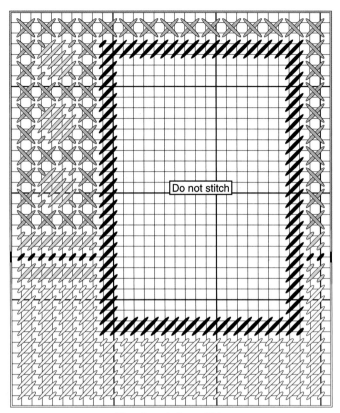

Live, Laugh, Love Side
31 holes x 37 holes
Cut 4 from stiff

COLOR KEY	
Yards	**Worsted Weight Yarn**
11 (10m)	■ Black #12
34 (31.1m)	☐ Eggshell #111
22 (20.1m)	▨ Warm brown #336
	⅛-Inch (4mm) Metallic Needlepoint Yarn
7 (6.4m)	☐ Gold #PC1
	6-Strand Embroidery Floss
4 (3.6m)	⁄ Black #310 (6-strand)
	Backstitch and Straight Stitch
	● Black #310 (6-strand) French Knot

Color numbers given are for Coats & Clark Red Heart Classic
worsted weight yarn Art. E267, Rainbow Gallery Plastic Canvas
7 Metallic Needlepoint Yarn and DMC 6-strand embroidery
floss.

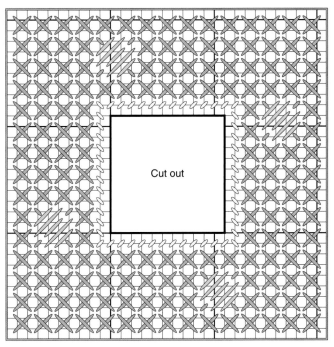

Live, Laugh, Love Top
31 holes x 31 holes
Cut 1 from stiff

COLOR KEY	
Yards	**Worsted Weight Yarn**
11 (10m)	■ Black #12
34 (31.1m)	☐ Eggshell #111
22 (20.1m)	▧ Warm brown #336
	⅛-Inch (4mm) Metallic Needlepoint Yarn
7 (6.4m)	☐ Gold #PC1
	6-Strand Embroidery Floss
4 (3.6m)	╱ Black #310 (6-strand) Backstitch and Straight Stitch
	● Black #310 (6-strand) French Knot

Color numbers given are for Coats & Clark Red Heart Classic worsted weight yarn Art. E267, Rainbow Gallery Plastic Canvas 7 Metallic Needlepoint Yarn and DMC 6-strand embroidery floss.

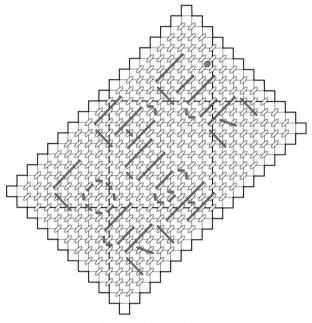

Live, Laugh, Love Sign
29 holes x 29 holes
Cut 4 from ivory

COLOR KEY	
Yards	**Worsted Weight Yarn**
11 (10m)	■ Black #12
34 (31.1m)	□ Eggshell #111
22 (20.1m)	▨ Warm brown #336
	⅛-Inch (4mm) Metallic Needlepoint Yarn
7 (6.4m)	▨ Gold #PC1
	6-Strand Embroidery Floss
4 (3.6m)	╱ Black #310 (6-strand)
	Backstitch and Straight Stitch
	● Black #310 (6-strand) French Knot

Color numbers given are for Coats & Clark Red Heart Classic worsted weight yarn Art. E267, Rainbow Gallery Plastic Canvas 7 Metallic Needlepoint Yarn and DMC 6-strand embroidery floss.

L-O-V-E

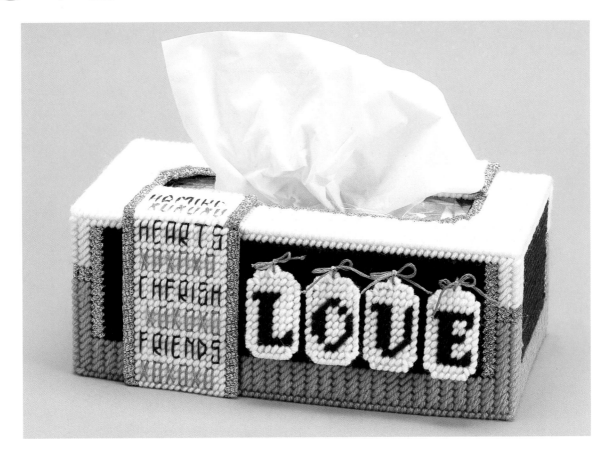

Size: 10 inches W x 3½ inches H x 5 inches deep
(25.4cm x 8.9cm x 12.7cm)
Skill Level: Intermediate

Materials

❏ 2 sheets stiff 7-count plastic canvas
❏ Coats & Clark Red Heart Classic worsted weight
   yarn Art. E267 as listed in color key
❏ Coats & Clark Red Heart Super Saver worsted
   weight yarn Art. E300 as listed in color key
❏ ⅛-inch (4mm) Plastic Canvas 7 Metallic
   Needlepoint Yarn from Rainbow Gallery as listed in
   color key
❏ DMC 6-strand embroidery floss as listed in color key
❏ Tapestry needles: #16 and #18
❏ Hot-glue gun and glue stick
❏ Fabric adhesive

Stitching Step By Step

1 Cut plastic canvas according to graphs. Cut out
opening in top.

2 Stitch sides, ends and top, leaving areas indicated on
top and sides unstitched.

3 Whipstitch sides and ends to top and to each other
along corners according to graphs. Overcast opening
in top, working white yarn over edge, and working
yellow gold metallic yarn over two bars. Overcast bottom
according to graphs.

4 Stitch lettering panels, working uncoded background
with white Continental Stitches. Whipstitch top and
side panels together in pairs; Overcast according to graphs,
working yellow gold metallic yarn over two bars.

5 Backstitch and Straight Stitch lettering on panels
using 6 strands mauve and very dark garnet
embroidery floss.

6 Glue lettering panels to tissue box using hot-glue gun.

7 Stitch tags, working uncoded background with white
Continental Stitches; Overcast according to graphs.

8 Cut four 12-inch lengths of mauve 6-strand
embroidery floss; use floss to tie tags to front of tissue
box where indicated by dots on graph for side. Knot ends of
floss; cut off excess. Secure knots with fabric adhesive.

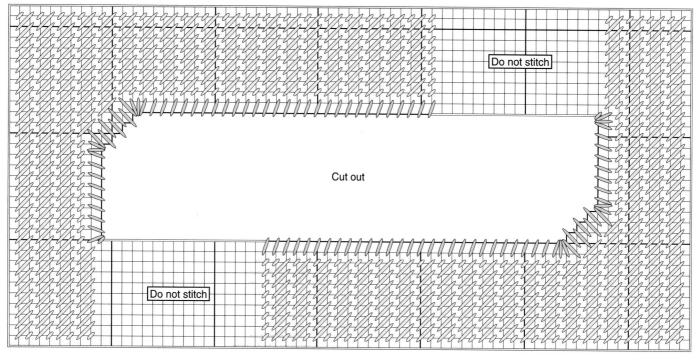

L-O-V-E Top
66 holes x 32 holes
Cut 1

COLOR KEY		
Yards	**Worsted Weight Yarn**	
23 (21m)	☐ Lily pink #719	
35 (32m)	■ Claret #762	
18 (16.4m)	☐ Light raspberry #774	
27 (24.7m)	Uncoded areas on lettering panels and tags are white #1 Continental Stitches	
	⁄ White #1 Overcasting and Whipstitching	
	⅛-Inch (4mm) Metallic Needlepoint Yarn	
16 (14.6m)	☐ Yellow gold #PC7	
	6-Strand Embroidery Floss	
6 (5.6m)	⁄ Very dark garnet #902 Backstitch and Straight Stitch	
8 (7.3m)	⁄ Mauve #3687 Backstitch and Straight Stitch	
	● Attach tag	

Color numbers given are for Coats & Clark Red Heart Classic worsted weight yarn Art. E267 and Super Saver worsted weight yarn Art. E300, Rainbow Gallery Plastic Canvas 7 Metallic Needlepoint Yarn and DMC 6-strand embroidery floss.

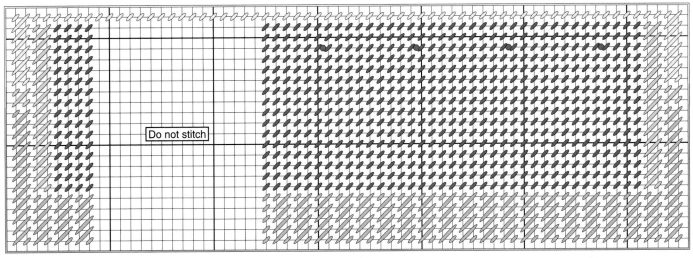

L-O-V-E Side
66 holes x 23 holes
Cut 2

COLOR KEY

Yards	Worsted Weight Yarn
23 (21m)	☐ Lily pink #719
35 (32m)	■ Claret #762
18 (16.4m)	▨ Light raspberry #774
27 (24.7m)	Uncoded areas on lettering panels and tags are white #1 Continental Stitches
	⁄ White #1 Overcasting and Whipstitching
	¹/₈-Inch (4mm) Metallic Needlepoint Yarn
16 (14.6m)	☐ Yellow gold #PC7
	6-Strand Embroidery Floss
6 (5.6m)	⁄ Very dark garnet #902 Backstitch and Straight Stitch
8 (7.3m)	⁄ Mauve #3687 Backstitch and Straight Stitch
	● Attach tag

Color numbers given are for Coats & Clark Red Heart Classic worsted weight yarn Art. E267 and Super Saver worsted weight yarn Art. E300, Rainbow Gallery Plastic Canvas 7 Metallic Needlepoint Yarn and DMC 6-strand embroidery floss.

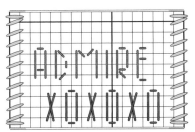

L-O-V-E Lettering Top Panel
17 holes x 11 holes
Cut 2

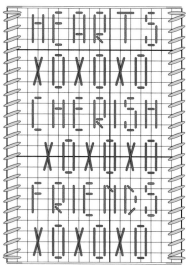

L-O-V-E Lettering Side Panel
17 holes x 24 holes
Cut 2

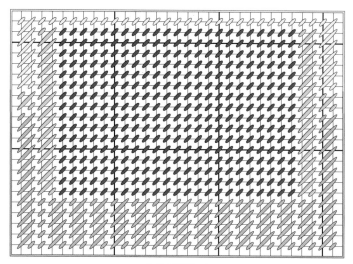

L-O-V-E End
32 holes x 23 holes
Cut 2

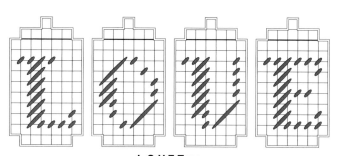

L-O-V-E Tags
7 holes x 12 holes each
Cut 1 each

COLOR KEY

Yards	Worsted Weight Yarn
23 (21m)	☐ Lily pink #719
35 (32m)	■ Claret #762
18 (16.4m)	▨ Light raspberry #774
27 (24.7m)	Uncoded areas on lettering panels and tags are white #1 Continental Stitches
	⁄ White #1 Overcasting and Whipstitching
	⅛-Inch (4mm) Metallic Needlepoint Yarn
16 (14.6m)	☐ Yellow gold #PC7
	6-Strand Embroidery Floss
6 (5.6m)	⁄ Very dark garnet #902 Backstitch and Straight Stitch
8 (7.3m)	⁄ Mauve #3687 Backstitch and Straight Stitch
	● Attach tag

Color numbers given are for Coats & Clark Red Heart Classic worsted weight yarn Art. E267 and Super Saver worsted weight yarn Art. E300, Rainbow Gallery Plastic Canvas 7 Metallic Needlepoint Yarn and DMC 6-strand embroidery floss.

Metro Stripe

Size: 4¾ inches W x 5½ inches H x 4¾ inches deep
(12.1cm x 14cm x 12.1cm)
Skill Level: Intermediate

Materials

- ❏ 2 sheets stiff 7-count plastic canvas
- ❏ Coats & Clark Red Heart Classic worsted weight yarn Art. E267 as listed in color key
- ❏ DMC 6-strand embroidery floss as listed in color key
- ❏ Tapestry needles: #16 and #18
- ❏ Hot-glue gun and glue sticks

Stitching Step By Step

1 Cut plastic canvas according to graphs. Cut out opening in top.

2 Stitch sides, top and flower panels. Overcast opening in top.

3 When background stitching is complete, add parakeet French Knots to flower centers. Straight Stitch flower stems using 6 strands black embroidery floss; Backstitch and Straight Stitch lettering using 6 strands red floss; Straight Stitch stripes on black areas using 3 strands white floss.

4 Whipstitch sides to top and to each other along corners according to graphs; Overcast bottom edge.

5 Overcast flower panels according to graphs; hot-glue panels over unstitched areas on sides.

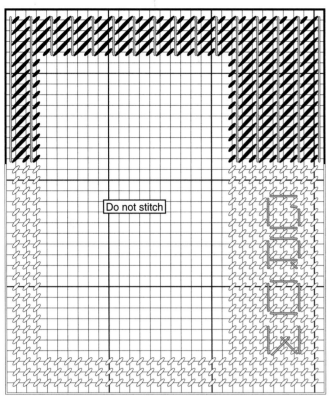

Metro Stripe Side
31 holes x 36 holes
Cut 4

Do not stitch

COLOR KEY

Yards	Worsted Weight Yarn
40 (36.6m)	☐ White #1
33 (30.2m)	■ Black #12
18 (16.4m)	☐ Parakeet #513
4 (3.6m)	■ Country red #914
	○ Parakeet #513 French Knot
	6-Strand Embroidery Floss
5 (4.7m)	✐ White (3-strand) Straight Stitch
3 (2.7m)	✐ Black #310 (6-strand) Straight Stitch
3 (2.7m)	✐ Red #321 (6-strand) Backstitch and Straight Stitch

Color numbers given are for Coats & Clark Red Heart Classic worsted weight yarn Art. E267 and DMC 6-strand embroidery floss.

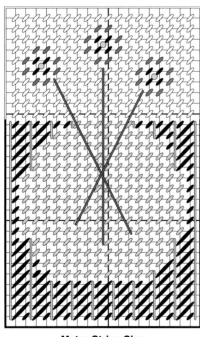

Metro Stripe Sign
19 holes x 30 holes
Cut 4

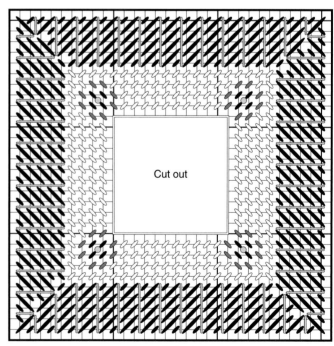

Cut out

Metro Stripe Top
31 holes x 31 holes
Cut 1

Flower Power

Size: 5 inches W x 5⅝ inches H x 5 inches deep
(12.7cm x 14.3cm x 12.7cm)

Skill Level: Intermediate

Materials

- ❑ 1½ sheets stiff 7-count plastic canvas
- ❑ Coats & Clark Red Heart Classic worsted weight yarn Art. E267 as listed in color key
- ❑ Coats & Clark Red Heart Kids worsted weight yarn Art. E711 as listed in color key
- ❑ #16 tapestry needle
- ❑ Hot-glue gun and glue sticks

Stitching Step By Step

1 Cut plastic canvas according to graphs. Cut out opening in top.

2 Stitch sides, top and squares according to graphs. Overcast opening in top.

3 When background stitching is complete, add pink and orange French Knots to flower centers on sides, top and squares. Add white Straight Stitches in corners on top; add red Straight Stitches and white Lazy Daisy Stitches on squares.

4 Whipstitch sides to top and to each other along corners according to graphs; Overcast bottom edge.

5 Overcast squares according to graphs; hot-glue squares over unstitched areas on sides.

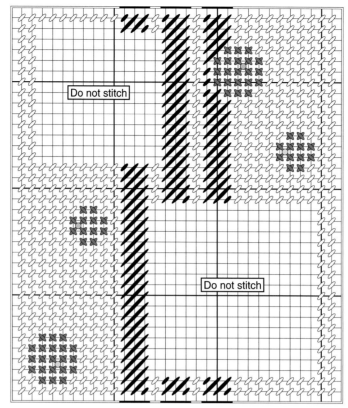

Flower Power Side
32 holes x 37 holes
Cut 4

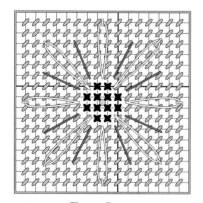

Flower Power
Large Flower Square
17 holes x 17 holes
Cut 4

COLOR KEY

Yards	Worsted Weight Yarn
44 (40.2m)	☐ White #1
21 (19.2m)	■ Black #12
20 (18.3m)	☐ Orange #2252
14 (12.8m)	☐ Red #2390
12 (11m)	☐ Pink #2734
	⟋ White #1 Straight Stitch
	⟋ Red #2390 Straight Stitch
	◉ Orange #2252 French Knot
	○ Pink #2734 French Knot
	⬭ White #1 Lazy Daisy Stitch

Color numbers given are for Coats & Clark Red Heart Classic worsted weight yarn Art. E267 and Kids worsted weight yarn Art. E711.

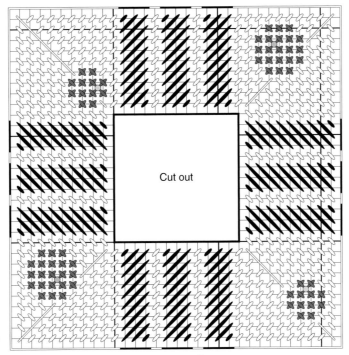

Flower Power Top
32 holes x 32 holes
Cut 1

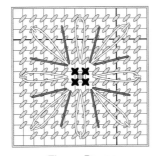

**Flower Power
Small Flower Square**
13 holes x 13 holes
Cut 4

COLOR KEY

Yards	Worsted Weight Yarn
44 (40.2m)	☐ White #1
21 (19.2m)	■ Black #12
20 (18.3m)	☐ Orange #2252
14 (12.8m)	■ Red #2390
12 (11m)	☐ Pink #2734
	╱ White #1 Straight Stitch
	╱ Red #2390 Straight Stitch
	● Orange #2252 French Knot
	○ Pink #2734 French Knot
	◔ White #1 Lazy Daisy Stitch

Color numbers given are for Coats & Clark Red Heart Classic worsted weight yarn Art. E267 and Kids worsted weight yarn Art. E711.

Retro Dots

Size: 9¾ inches W x 5 inches H x 3⅞ inches deep
(24.8cm x 12.7cm x 9.8cm)
Skill Level: Intermediate

Materials

❏ 1½ sheets stiff 7-count plastic canvas
❏ Coats & Clark Red Heart Classic worsted weight
yarn Art. E267 as listed in color key
❏ Coats & Clark Red Heart Super Saver worsted
weight yarn Art. E300 as listed in color key
❏ #16 tapestry needle

Stitching Step By Step

1 Cut plastic canvas according to graphs. Cut out opening in top.

2 Stitch sides, ends and top, working uncoded areas with soft white Continental Stitches. Overcast opening in top.

3 Whipstitch sides and ends to top and to each other along corners according to graphs; Overcast bottom edge.

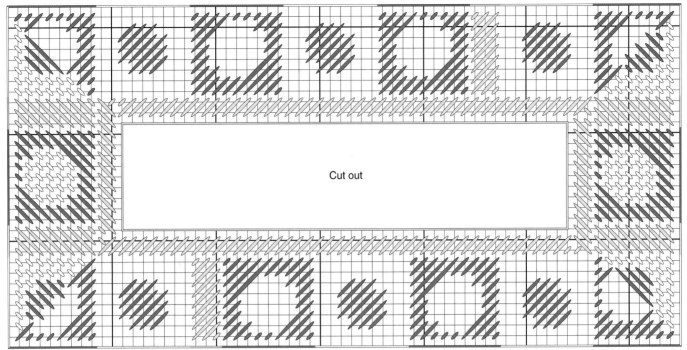

Retro Dots Top
65 holes x 32 holes
Cut 1

COLOR KEY

Yards	Worsted Weight Yarn
45 (41.1m)	☐ Soft white #316
42 (38.4m)	■ Coffee #365
15 (13.7m)	☐ Blue jewel #818

Uncoded areas are soft white
#316 Continental Stitches
Color numbers given are for Coats & Clark Red
Heart Classic worsted weight yarn Art. E267 and
Super Saver worsted weight yarn Art. E300.

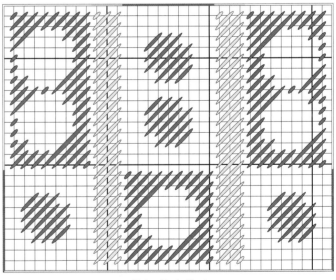

Retro Dots End
32 holes x 25 holes
Cut 2

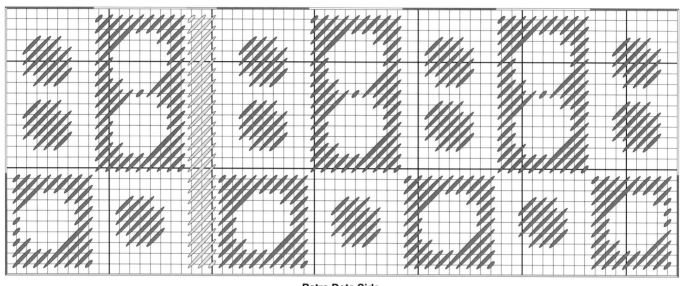

Retro Dots Side
65 holes x 25 holes
Cut 2

COLOR KEY	
Yards	**Worsted Weight Yarn**
45 (41.1m)	☐ Soft white #316
42 (38.4m)	■ Coffee #365
15 (13.7m)	☐ Blue jewel #818
	Uncoded areas are soft white
	#316 Continental Stitches

Color numbers given are for Coats & Clark Red Heart Classic worsted weight yarn Art. E267 and Super Saver worsted weight yarn Art. E300.

Inspire

Size: 5 inches W x 5 ⅝ inches H x 5 inches deep
(12.7cm x 14.3cm x 12.7cm)

Skill Level: Intermediate

Materials

❏ 1½ sheets stiff 7-count plastic canvas
❏ Coats & Clark Red Heart Classic worsted weight yarn Art. E267 as listed in color key
❏ DMC 6-strand embroidery floss as listed in color key
❏ Tapestry needles: #16 and #18

Stitching Step By Step

1 Cut plastic canvas according to graphs. Cut out opening in top.

2 Stitch Slanted Gobelin and Continental stitches on sides and top according to graphs. Long Stitch white flowers using 2 strands white yarn. Overcast opening in top.

3 When background stitching is complete, Backstitch and Straight Stitch lettering and flower stems using 6 strands black embroidery floss.

4 Whipstitch sides to top and to each other along corners according to graphs; Overcast bottom edge.

5 Attach signs to sides, working large diagonal stitches at corners with 6 strands black embroidery floss.

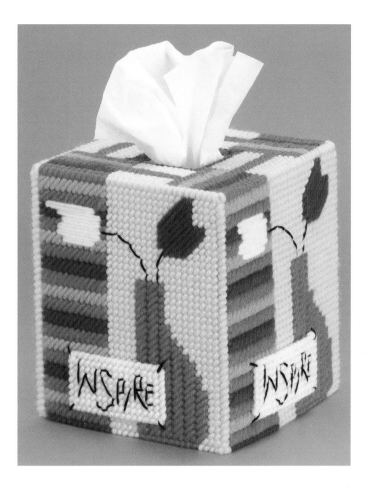

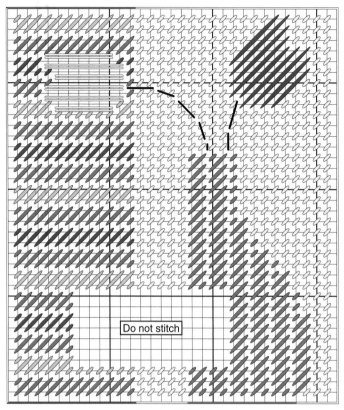

Inspire Side
32 holes x 37 holes
Cut 4

Do not stitch

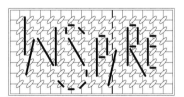

Inspire Sign
16 holes x 8 holes
Cut 4

COLOR KEY

Yards	Worsted Weight Yarn
15 (13.7m)	☐ White #1
42 (38.4m)	☐ Sea coral #246
12 (11m)	▨ Medium coral #252
35 (32m)	▦ Country red #914
17 (15.5m)	■ Cardinal #917
	⟋ White #1 Long Stitch
	6-Strand Embroidery Floss
7 (6.4m)	✎ Black #310 (6-strand)
	Backstitch and Straight Stitch

Color numbers given are for Coats & Clark Red Heart Classic worsted weight yarn Art. E267 and DMC 6-strand embroidery floss.

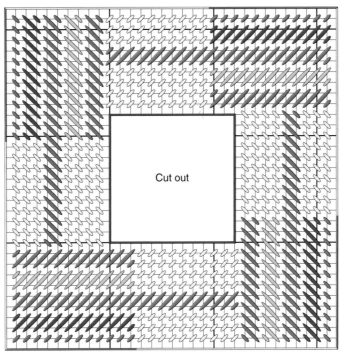

Inspire Top
32 holes x 32 holes
Cut 1

COLOR KEY	
Yards	**Worsted Weight Yarn**
15 (13.7m)	☐ White #1
42 (38.4m)	☐ Sea coral #246
12 (11m)	☐ Medium coral #252
35 (32m)	☐ Country red #914
17 (15.5m)	■ Cardinal #917
	⁄ White #1 Long Stitch
	6-Strand Embroidery Floss
7 (6.4m)	⁄ Black #310 (6-strand)
	Backstitch and Straight Stitch

Color numbers given are for Coats & Clark Red Heart Classic worsted weight yarn Art. E267 and DMC 6-strand embroidery floss.

306 E. Parr Road
Berne, IN 46711
www.NeedlecraftShop.com
© 2005 The Needlecraft Shop

The full line of The Needlecraft Shop
products is carried by Annie's Attic catalog.
TOLL-FREE ORDER LINE
or to request a free catalog
(800) 582-6643
Customer Service
(800) 449-0440
Fax (800) 882-6643
Visit www.AnniesAttic.com

ISBN-10: 1-57367-203-3

ISBN-13: 978-1-57367-203-0

All rights reserved.

Printed in USA

2 3 4 5 6 7 8 9

Shopping for Supplies

For supplies, first shop your local craft
and needlework stores. Some supplies
may be found in fabric, hardware and
discount stores. If you are unable to find
the supplies you need, please call Annie's
Attic at (800) 259-4000 to request a free
catalog that sells plastic canvas supplies.

Getting Started

Before You Cut

Buy one brand of canvas for each entire project, as brands can dif-
fer slightly in the distance between bars. Count holes carefully from the
graph before you cut, using the bolder lines that show each 10 holes.
These 10-mesh lines begin in the lower left corner of each graph to make
counting easier. Mark canvas before cutting, then remove all marks completely before stitching. If the piece is cut in a rectangular or square shape
and is either not worked, or worked with only one color and one type of
stitch, we do not include the graph in the pattern. Instead, we give the
cutting and stitching instructions in the general instructions or with the
individual project instructions.

Covering the Canvas

Bring needle up from back of work, leaving a short length of yarn on
back of canvas; work over short length to secure. To end a thread, weave
needle and thread through the wrong side of your last few stitches; clip.
Follow the numbers on the small graphs beside each stitch illustration; bring
your needle up from the back of the work on odd numbers and down through
the front of the work on even numbers. Work embroidery stitches last, after
the canvas has been completely covered by the needlepoint stitches.

Basic Stitches

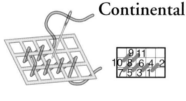

Continental   Overcast   Whipstitch

Slanted
Gobelin   Long   Cross

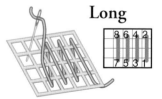 

Embroidery Stitches

French Knot   Lazy Daisy   Backstitch   Straight

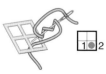    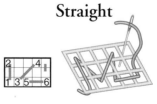

METRIC KEY:
millimeters = (mm)
centimeters = (cm)
meters = (m)
grams = (g)